This book belongs to

..................................................

Consultant Sarah Davis is a (UKCP Registered) psychotherapist with an MA in Integrative Child and Adolescent Psychotherapy and Counseling.

She currently works in the voluntary sector, counseling and supporting young people to improve their mental wellbeing. She has also worked as a children's editor and consultant.

Published in 2022 by Welbeck Children's Books
An imprint of Welbeck Children's Limited, part of Welbeck Publishing Group.
Based in London and Sydney
www.welbeckpublishing.com

Text and illustrations © Welbeck Children's Limited,
part of Welbeck Publishing Group.

*Art Director:* Margaret Hope
*Designer:* Nancy Leschnikoff
*Editor:* Jenni Lazell

ISBN 978-1-78312-754-2

Printed in Dongguan, China

10 9 8 7 6 5 4 3 2 1

# Find your HAPPY

Catherine Veitch, with
Sarah Davis, child and adolescent psychotherapist
Illustrated by Jessica Smith

WELBECK

# CONTENTS

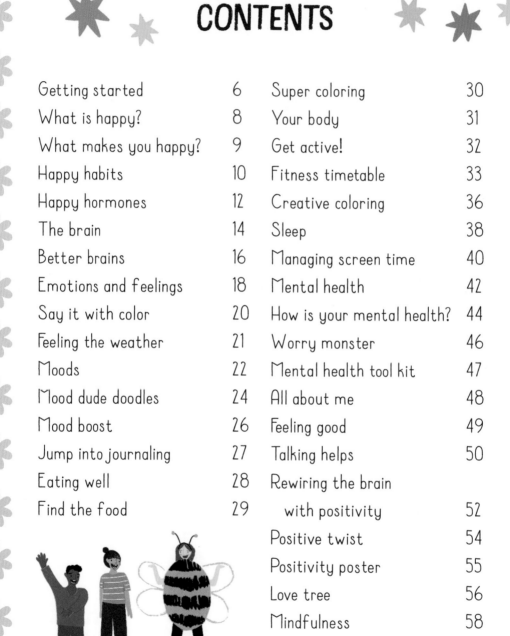

I LOVE ME!

# GETTING STARTED

This book is full of ideas and activities to help improve your happiness. You can work through them in order or pick out pages at random, depending on how you feel. Before you start, here's a quick introduction to the topic of happiness.

The term "happiness" means different things to different people. It can be experienced as a feeling of joy in the moment, a sense of longer-term satisfaction in life, or a sense of having more positive than negative emotions. But where does it begin and how do we find it?

It starts with your relationships with your parents and caregivers. This first relationship has enormous influence in shaping your self-esteem, expectations of other people, and view of the world in general. And it creates a safe base from which you can go out into the world and find fulfilment. But other factors are important too—genetics, life events and circumstances, and the ability and opportunity to succeed at your passions and be recognized for them, all add to the secret "happiness sauce."

Though we can't control all the factors that contribute to happiness, there are plenty that we can! Scientists have discovered that doing activities that release "happy hormones" into our brains, such as eating well, exercising, and pursuing goals and dreams, are great ways to work towards contentment. It turns out that having huge, belly-laughing, raucous fun with people we love and who love us, is really good for us.

Of course, there are times when we do not feel happy, our mental health suffers, and we can't find those wonderful light moments that make us smile, laugh, and connect with others. This is also normal and an everyday part of life. In these harder moments we can learn to reach out to people to support us, carry on with our "happy habits" until they make us feel good again, and—most importantly—be patient and kind to ourselves.

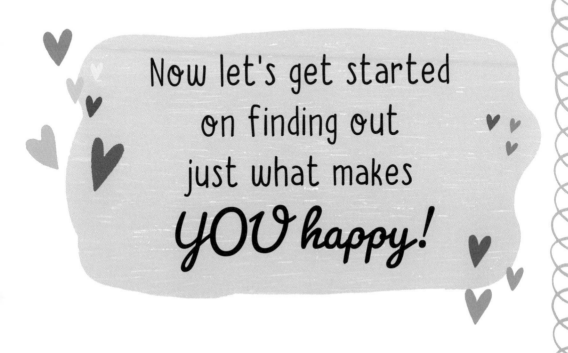

Now let's get started
on finding out
just what makes
*YOU happy!*

# WHAT IS HAPPY?

Being happy is a nice feeling. But what is happy?

You can see people are happy by their expressions and the ways they move. You can also hear people are happy through the sound of their voices: some have big belly laughs, and others, infectious giggles. What do your friends and family, and even your pets, look and sound like when they are happy?

Can you feel happiness? It may be soft and fluffy, or crunchy and crinkly. What smells mean happiness to you? Is it the sweet fragrance of a flower or the smell of your favorite dinner, or maybe it's your grandmother's hug?

There are no wrong answers. Happiness looks, sounds, feels, and smells differently for us all.

*Circle all the words that describe how you feel when you are happy, and add some words of your own if they are missing.*

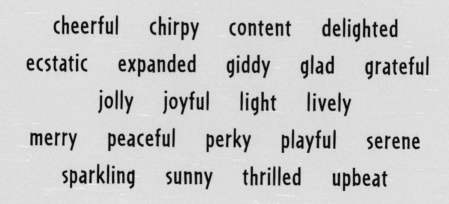

cheerful   chirpy   content   delighted
ecstatic   expanded   giddy   glad   grateful
jolly   joyful   light   lively
merry   peaceful   perky   playful   serene
sparkling   sunny   thrilled   upbeat

----------------     ----------------     ----------------

# WHAT MAKES YOU HAPPY?

### Many things make us happy.

Sometimes other people do things that make us happy. Simple things such as smiling at us, or giving us praise. At other times we make ourselves happy working on a hobby or doing something well. Spending time with our friends and family can also make us feel happy.

Think of something recently that made you really happy. What were you doing? What did you feel like in that moment?

Here are some well-known sayings that describe what happiness feels like.

Flying High

WALKING ON AIR

ON CLOUD NINE

Floating on Air

Over the Moon

BURSTING WITH HAPPINESS

Make up a saying to describe what happiness feels like to you.

# HAPPY PEOPLE
# HAVE HAPPY HABITS

Have you found that if you practice something over and over again it gets easier to do, and after a while, you can do it without thinking? This is because it has become a habit.

It's important to work on happy habits, as the more you practice things that make you happy, the more you will develop happy habits, and the happier you will feel.

What happy habits can you practice? For example, what do you like to play, what exercises can you do, what healthy things can you eat? Think of a happy habit you could do for each of the topics below. Then fill in these shapes with your happy habit by writing or drawing a picture of it.

Playing    **EXERCISING    EATING HEALTHILY**

*DOING THINGS YOU LOVE*    Spending time with friends

Doing things for others    **SETTING GOALS**

**LOOKING FOR THE GOOD IN PEOPLE**

Why don't you ...

... make some Happy Habit shapes. Cut out some hearts or other shapes from colored paper or card and write or draw a happy habit inside each one. Decorate them and stick them up around your home to remind you to practice some happy habits.

SETTING GOALS

PLAYING

# HAPPY HORMONES

### Did you know that hormones in your body help you to feel happy?

Hormones are chemicals that are made in special organs in the body called the endocrine glands. These glands release hormones into your blood. The hormones then travel round your body like messengers, telling different parts, even tiny cells, to do things. For example, hormones tell your body when to grow and when to stop growing. They also control things such as your memory, digestion, sleep, and moods. Those hormones have a lot of power!

## Spreading Happiness

How do you feel when you do something you enjoy, such as playing football with a friend, or even just thinking of going out to play football? Do you feel a rush of happiness? This is because your brain has been flooded with the hormone dopamine. Your brain releases this hormone when it expects something happy, or a reward, and it makes you feel joyful and excited. Dopamine also helps you to learn, remember, and sleep well. It's easier to learn and remember things when you are happy. And it's easy to sleep after a day of excitement.

## Cuddletime

Does looking at a friend and sharing a smile, a cuddle with a loved one, or a snuggle with a pet make you feel safe, happy, and comfortable? This feeling is because your brain has released a hormone called oxytocin. This hormone is released when you make connections like this with other people, and even your pets, and it helps you to bond further.

## Multi-tasking

The last of our happy hormones is serotonin. This travels all over your body and helps to control many things, including your moods, sleep, and digestion. Serotonin helps you to feel happier, calmer, more focused, and less anxious. Sounds like a good all-rounder!

# THE BRAIN

To get a clearer idea of what happiness is, it will help to understand the science of how your brain actually works.

Your brain is like a big computer that never switches off. Even when you are fast asleep, your brain is busy sending and receiving messages to and from your senses and parts of your body, to keep you alive. But your brain can do so much more than a computer, as you think and experience emotions, like happiness, in your brain.

## A NEST OF NEURONS

From the outside, your brain looks like a giant walnut with lots of folds and creases. It's made up of billions of nerve cells called neurons. These neurons are connected to each other in a complex web and communicate at incredible speeds.

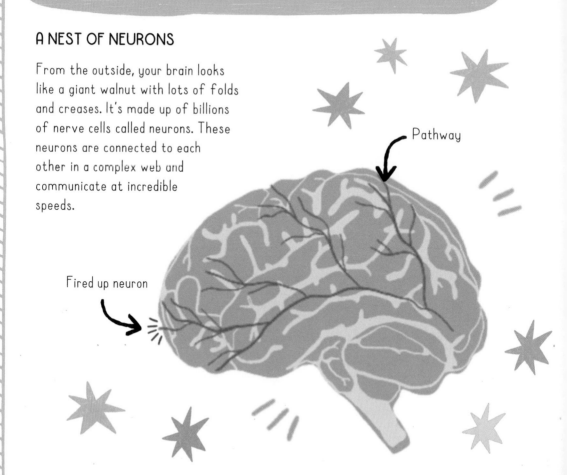

Pathway

Fired up neuron

## LIGHTNING-QUICK REACTIONS

In order to talk to each other, a neuron needs to be woken, or fired up. If it starts to rain when you are outside, senses in your skin feel the raindrops on your body and quickly send a message to your brain. This message fires up the necessary neurons that send messages out to parts of your body. For example, they may tell your hands to pull up your hood to keep you dry, or they may tell your legs to run for cover, or if you love getting wet, they may tell you to laugh. This all happens super-quick and you do it without thinking.

## BUILDING PATHWAYS

Messages travel in your brain along pathways. Every time you do something, billions of pathways light up in your brain. The brain is changeable (scientists call this *neuroplastic!*) and can create new pathways and connections all the time. It is good to create new pathways as they give you different ways of doing things and solving problems, and help your brain to grow. Every time you do something that makes you happy or something new, your brain creates new pathways. So being happy and trying new things increases your brain power!

# BETTER BRAINS

Let's create some new pathways in your brain right now by doing some new things. Don't worry, they don't have to be huge. Even small changes can make a difference in your brain.

## How to play

**1.** Write a new challenge on each of the Challenge Cards. It can be anything that is safe to do, but it must be something that you don't usually do.

**2.** Tear up some paper and cover each Challenge Card with a piece of paper.

**3.** Uncover a card at a time and do the challenge on the card.

*You could ask a friend or family member to write some, too, and take it in turns to do the challenges.*

**CHALLENGE CARD**

CHALLENGE CARD

Here are some examples to get you started:

☆ Throw and catch a ball in your non-dominant hand (the hand you don't use for writing).

☆ Say three sentences about yourself, adding the word "bobble" before every word.

☆ Stand on one leg and sing your favorite song.

CHALLENGE CARD

CHALLENGE CARD

CHALLENGE CARD

Challenge Card

CHALLENGE CARD

Challenge Card

# EMOTIONS AND FEELINGS

Emotions are instinctive, physical reactions that everyone shares. Feelings are the meaning you give to emotion and are influenced by your beliefs, memories, and life experiences.

Here are a few things you may feel for the emotions of rage, sadness, anxiety, and fear. Circle any feelings you have felt before.

| Rage | Sadness | Anxiety | Fear |
| --- | --- | --- | --- |
| angry | grief | uncertain | frightened |
| bitter | hurt | restless | anxious |
| furious | hopeless | doubt | worried |
| mad | miserable | dread | alarmed |
| resentful | gloomy | jitters | dread |
| jealous | cheerless | nervous | timid |

To understand our emotions better and also to help other people understand us, it helps to say how we are feeling. Next time you feel one of these emotions, try using one of the words in the list under it to describe how you are feeling.

## Ready for action

When we are under a lot of stress, we experience what scientists call "fight or flight." This is when organs in the body called the adrenal glands release the hormones adrenaline and noradrenaline. These hormones cause changes in our bodies. For example, we may notice our breathing and heartbeat speed up, our muscles tremble, and our pupils get bigger.

All of these changes are getting our bodies ready to fight whatever has frightened us or to run from it. This reaction can help you perform better under pressure, and in a life-threatening situation, it could help you to survive.

## Body check

When you feel emotions, your body reacts in many different ways. Where do you feel different emotions in your body? For example, you may clench your teeth, raise your shoulders, drop your head, or feel a knot in your tummy. Draw or write where and how you feel these different emotions in your body.

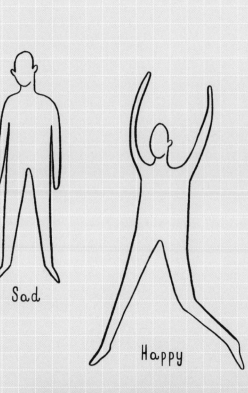

Sad

Happy

Anxious

Angry

We often try to bury uncomfortable feelings, instead of facing them. Why do you think it helps our mental health to face how we are feeling?

# SAY IT WITH COLOR

People sometimes use colors to show how they are feeling, with expressions such as "seeing red," "feeling blue," and "green with envy."

These aliens are from the Color Planet but—oh dear—since leaving their planet all their colors have disappeared! Draw lines to match each alien to a feeling. Then color them in, using a different color for each alien and emotion. There are no wrong answers. Think about how different colors make you feel.

You may find it useful to use colors to describe how you are feeling.

*happy*

**worried**

**SAD**

**SCARED**

Draw an expression and color this face to show how you are feeling.

# FEELING THE WEATHER

## How are you feeling today?

Are you feeling full of joy like a ray of sunshine, or are you angry with a face like thunder? People often use weather vocabulary to express how they are feeling. Make up some feelings to match each of these weather symbols.

*Draw a weather symbol to show how you are feeling today, and write a sentence about your feelings.*

----------------------------
----------------------------
----------------------------
----------------------------
----------------------------
----------------------------
----------------------------
----------------------------

## Why don't you ...

*...make a weather report for your feelings every day this week? At the end of the week, look at what things made you happy.*

Monday
Cloud and sunshine

# MOODS

Do you ever feel restless, irritable, sulky, or sour?
Have you ever snapped at someone for no reason?
The chances are you are in a bad mood, as our moods affect
our behavior. It's normal to have bad moods sometimes,
just as it's normal to also have good moods.

## HELPFUL HAND

Being around people in a bad mood may make you feel
down, too. But, if you notice one of your friends or
family are in a bad mood, don't judge them, as it may
be because of one of the triggers on the next page.
Ask them if they are okay. Sometimes showing someone
you care is a kind gift, which helps to lift their mood.

## BAD MOOD TRIGGERS

☆ Feeling stressed or worried about something.
☆ Upset with a friend or family member.
☆ Not eating a healthy diet.
☆ Feeling hungry.
☆ Not enough sleep.
☆ Feeling bored.

## MAKING CHANGES

It helps to understand when we are in a bad mood and what causes it, as then we can try to make changes to stop it. For example: we can learn ways to help us cope with stress better; we can make healthy changes to our diet; we can change our night-time routine to get more sleep; we can look at something in a different way to make it more interesting, or do some exercises to wake up our bodies.

## MOOD SWINGS

Changes in moods are normal, especially as you grow older, but if you find that your feelings and behavior are extreme, you may be suffering from mood swings and could need some help to manage them. Talk to a parent, caregiver, or a teacher about it.

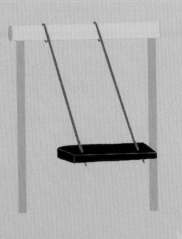

GOOD MOOD

BAD MOOD

# MOOD DUDE DOODLES

Meet the Mood Dude Doodles. Can you tell who is in a bad mood, and who is in a good mood? Read the reasons why in their speech bubbles.

*Over the next few days draw some of your own Mood Dude Doodles (you can copy these or invent your own characters) to show your moods.*

Remember to give them expressions to show how you are feeling, and write why in their speech bubbles.

When you've finished your doodles, look at the things that put you in a good or a bad mood. What can you do to change the things that put you in a bad mood? Can you do more of the things that put you in a good mood?

# MOOD BOOST

Here are some things you can do right now to turn up the temperature and boost your mood.

The next time you feel in a bad mood, give them a try and see if they work. Then color in the mood thermometer to show how happy you are.

**Listen to MUSIC...**
- ☆ Gentle music calms us down
- ☆ Lively music cheers us up
- ☆ Songs remind us of happy times

**LAUGH out loud...**
- ➡ We feel better after a giggle with friends
- ➡ Watch or listen to something funny
- ➡ Share some jokes

**Try to LOOK ON THE BRIGHT SIDE...**
- ☆ Think of things you are grateful for
- ☆ Think of things you like about yourself
- ☆ Think of things you like about other people

**Decide to be HAPPY...**
- ➡ Think happy thoughts
- ➡ Say happy words
- ➡ Do things that make you happy

*a happy bunny*

*feeling brighter*

*OK*

*out of sorts*

*down in the dumps*

**Do a GOOD DEED**
**for someone else...**
- ☆ You will feel much happier
- ☆ It will help you to forget about your problems
- ☆ Spread happiness by smiling at people

*Do you do something else to boost your mood? Write it down here.*

\- \- \- \- \- \- \- \-
\- \- \- \- \- \- \- \-
\- \- \- \- \- \- \- \-
\- \- \- \- \- \- \- \-
\- \- \- \- \- \- \- \-
\- \- \- \- \- \- \- \-
\- \- \- \- \- \- \- \-

# JUMP INTO JOURNALING

A journal is like a diary, only rather than writing about things you do, you write down your thoughts and how you feel about things.

Journaling is a great way to keep track of your moods and to let feelings out. You can also remind yourself of things you can be proud of. Give yourself 5 or 10 minutes and write down anything that comes to mind. Don't worry about spelling or grammar. Just let it all out.

If you're not used to journaling, you may find it hard at first, but the more often you journal, the easier it becomes.

# EATING WELL

There is some truth in the saying "You are what you eat," as eating a healthy diet gives us a healthy body, and a healthy body lifts our mood and makes us feel happy.

Plenty of water and a balanced diet that includes all of the foods on the plate is a healthy diet. The bigger the section, the more you can eat of those foods.

*Choose higher fiber wholegrain foods, such as wholewheat pasta and brown rice.*

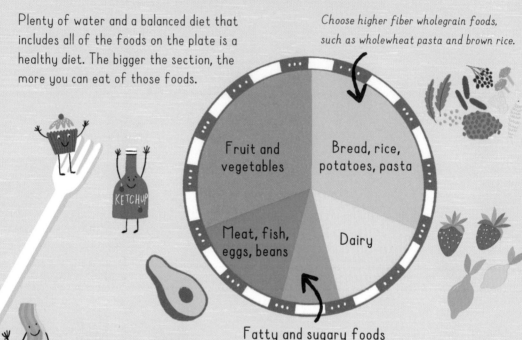

Fruit and vegetables

Bread, rice, potatoes, pasta

Meat, fish, eggs, beans

Dairy

Fatty and sugary foods

## NAUGHTY FOODS

Eating too much fatty, salty and sugary foods is not good for our bodies and can make us feel heavy, tired and crabby. It is better for your body to only eat these foods in small amounts.

## HEALTHY EATING HABITS

☆ It's easier to eat healthily if others around you eat healthy food, too. Ask your family and friends to eat healthy food with you.

☆ Ask a parent or carer if you can cook or prepare food together. It's fun, and feels great eating food that you have helped to cook.

# FIND THE FOOD

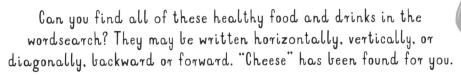

Can you find all of these healthy food and drinks in the wordsearch? They may be written horizontally, vertically, or diagonally, backward or forward. "Cheese" has been found for you.

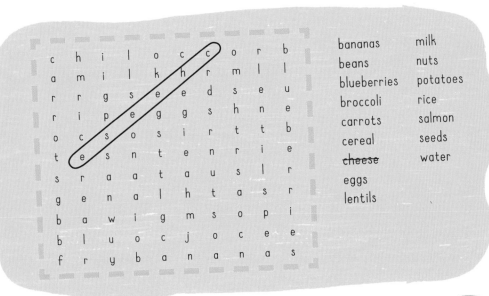

```
c  h  i  l  o  c  c  o  r  b
a  m  i  l  k  h  r  m  l  l
r  r  g  s  e  e  d  s  e  u
r  i  p  e  g  g  s  h  n  e
o  c  s  o  s  i  r  t  t  b
t  e  s  n  t  e  n  r  i  e
s  r  a  a  t  a  u  s  l  r
g  e  n  a  l  h  t  a  s  r
b  a  w  i  g  m  s  o  p  i
b  l  u  o  c  j  o  c  e  e
f  r  y  b  a  n  a  n  a  s
```

bananas
beans
blueberries
broccoli
carrots
cereal
~~cheese~~
eggs
lentils

milk
nuts
potatoes
rice
salmon
seeds
water

## PLAN A HEALTHY MEAL

*Draw and color a healthy meal and drink using some of the food and drinks above, and add any other healthy food you can think of.*

# SUPER COLORING

Foods packed with nutrients (that's the good stuff
our bodies need to live and grow) are super-healthy
for our bodies and minds.

*These foods have been nicknamed superfoods.
Color in these superfoods with your super colors.*

*Do you know any other superfoods?
If not, can you find out?*

# YOUR BODY

Everyone's body is different and we all need different things. But looking after your body and keeping fit will help you to keep healthy and happy.

## TAKE CARE

Have you noticed how taking care of your body can feel good? Things like feeling clean after a shower, putting on fresh clothes and brushing your teeth? Taking care of yourself also includes keeping your body safe, such as wrapping up warm in cold weather. Caring for our bodies shows we value and respect them.

## OUTSTANDING PERFORMANCE

Exercise helps us to grow strong and healthy by building stronger hearts, bones and muscles, and improving our posture and balance. A strong, healthy body also builds our self-esteem.

## MOOD BOOST

Do you feel amazing after exercising? When you exercise, your brain releases chemicals called endorphins, which make you feel good. So exercise is good for your mind, too! Aerobic exercises (the ones that get your heart pumping) will actually help your brain cells to grow and create new pathways and connections in your brain.

# GET ACTIVE!

It's time to get active. Make an aerobic exercise spinner,
then follow the rules for the game.

## Make an aerobic exercise spinner

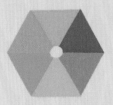

**1.** Draw a large hexagon onto card, such as the inside of a cereal box. Divide it into six segments and add a small circle in the middle, as in the picture. Cut it out.

**2.** Draw or write the name of an aerobic exercise in each segment. Choose some of the exercises given or add some of your own.

**3.** Push a pencil through the center.

## How to play

1  Gently shake your arms and legs, and jiggle about to warm up before you begin.
2  Spin the spinner and do the aerobic exercise it lands on for a set time.
   Repeat the moves, changing arms or legs. Start with exercising for however long you are comfortable, and increase the time as you play the game more often.
3  Do some gentle stretches to finish. Repeat steps 1 to 3 for some more exercises.

## TOP TRAINING TIPS

☆ If an exercise is uncomfortable or causes you pain, stop immediately.
☆ Wear comfortable clothes in layers that you can peel off if you get hot.
☆ Drink plenty of water.

# FITNESS TIMETABLE

It is good for our bodies and minds if we make
keeping active a happy habit every day.

What exercises do you like doing? You may play a sport, love dancing or
riding your bike, or just enjoy running around playing games. Fill in your
fitness timetable by writing an exercise you can do each day this week.
Then tick the box when you have done it and write how you felt afterwards.

| | My exercise | I did it! | How it made me feel... |
|---|---|---|---|
| Monday | | | |
| Tuesday | | | |
| Wednesday | | | |
| Thursday | | | |
| Friday | | | |
| Saturday | | | |
| Sunday | | | |

### DID YOU KNOW
If you find it difficult to stick to a timetable, tell someone
supportive what you're doing and ask them to remind you
about your fitness challenge—or do it with you!

*" If you have good thoughts they will shine out of your face like sunbeams and you will always look lovely."*

from Roald Dahl's
The Twits

Let your mind wander and fill this space with happy things.

# CREATIVE COLORING

Be creative with your colors and enjoy the moment.

# SLEEP

If you don't get much sleep do you feel cranky and snappy in the morning? How much sleep we get can affect our mood. Sleep is vital for feeling good, as when we sleep, our body recharges and heals.

When you sleep, your body releases hormones that slow down your breathing and relax other muscles in your body. The body can then repair any damage, such as swelling (called inflammation), caused by daily wear and tear.

## TOSSING AND TURNING
It's not always easy to fall asleep and to get a good 10 to 11 hours of sleep a night. Sometimes things may keep you awake. Eating a big meal just before bedtime, noisy neighbors, or worries on your mind may make you restless. Here are some things you can do that may help you to sleep.

# TIPS FOR A SWEET SLEEP

Talk about your worries to a parent or a caregiver, or even a friend.

Make your bedroom a comfortable place to sleep in.

Set a bedtime routine, going to bed at a similar time each night.

Exercise regularly, but not too close to bedtime.

Try not to eat or drink too much too close to bedtime.

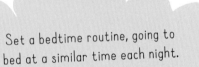

Focus on doing calm things before bedtime, such as reading.

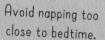

Avoid looking at screens too close to bedtime.

Avoid napping too close to bedtime.

If you have tried these and still have problems sleeping, speak to a trusted grown-up, as you may need help from a doctor.

# MANAGING SCREEN TIME

Do you spend too much time looking at a screen?
Staring at our phones and TVs can lead to problems
with your mental and physical health.

## SCREEN OVERLOAD

Did you know, too much screen time
can lead to problems with sleep, paying
attention, and even depression, anxiety,
and obesity. Screens can upset our
sleep, as their blue light stops our
bodies from making a hormone called
melatonin, which we need to control our
sleeping and waking. Sitting at a screen
for a long time, instead of being active,
can also lead to obesity.

## TAKE CARE
It is important to be safe online. Ask a parent,
caregiver or teacher for guidance and talk to
them if you are worried about anything you
see online.

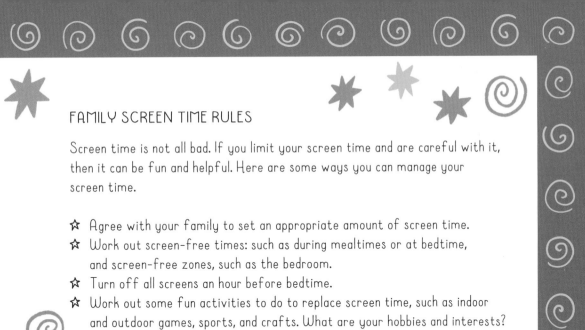

## FAMILY SCREEN TIME RULES

Screen time is not all bad. If you limit your screen time and are careful with it, then it can be fun and helpful. Here are some ways you can manage your screen time.

☆ Agree with your family to set an appropriate amount of screen time.
☆ Work out screen-free times: such as during mealtimes or at bedtime, and screen-free zones, such as the bedroom.
☆ Turn off all screens an hour before bedtime.
☆ Work out some fun activities to do to replace screen time, such as indoor and outdoor games, sports, and crafts. What are your hobbies and interests? Are there clubs you can join?

### MY SCREEN RULES

Think about how you can manage your screen time, and talk to an adult about it so you can together come up with a list of ten screen rules that you and the whole family can follow.

1.
2.
3.
4.
5.
6.
7.
8.
9.
10.

# MENTAL HEALTH

Our mental health is just as important as our physical health, as it affects how we think, act, and feel. Some people refer to our mental health as our wellbeing.

## WHAT IS MENTAL HEALTH?

Being mentally healthy means that we feel good about ourselves, have positive relationships with others, and can feel and manage all our varied emotions.

## BOUNCING BACK

We all have times when we feel stressed and frightened. Good mental health helps us to cope with these ups and downs, by dealing with our emotions and being in control of our lives. It helps us to accept how we are feeling at the time, but to realize that those feelings will pass. Good mental health also allows us to ask for help from others when we need support.

# HOW MENTAL HEALTH CAN CHANGE

It's important to regularly check in with how we are feeling as our mental health doesn't always stay the same. It can change as things in our lives change. For example, events such as moving school or home, bullying, the death of a loved one, not fitting in, illness, or parents splitting up can all affect our mental wellbeing.

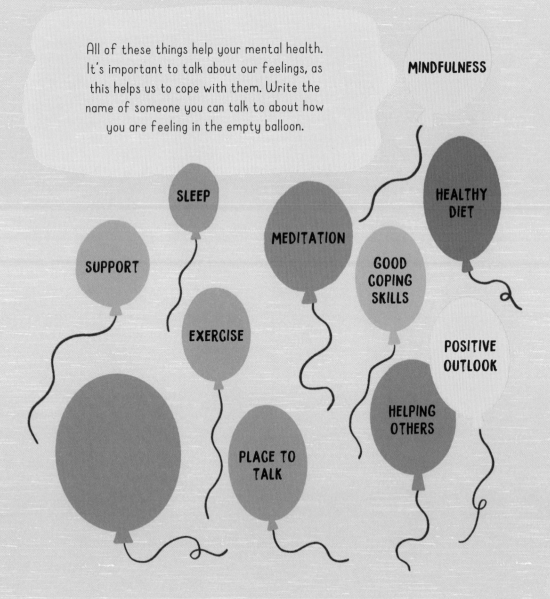

All of these things help your mental health. It's important to talk about our feelings, as this helps us to cope with them. Write the name of someone you can talk to about how you are feeling in the empty balloon.

MINDFULNESS

SLEEP

MEDITATION

HEALTHY DIET

SUPPORT

GOOD COPING SKILLS

EXERCISE

POSITIVE OUTLOOK

HELPING OTHERS

PLACE TO TALK

# HOW IS YOUR MENTAL HEALTH?

It's time to stop and think about your mental health.

Write ten things you have done today in the stopwatch. You may want to include quick things such as brushing your teeth and chatting to family, or longer things, such as games you've played or your school work. It's up to you.

When you've filled in the stopwatch think carefully about how you felt when you did each thing. Color the segment in red if you felt anxious or stressed, color the segment in green if you felt calm or happy. Then write the number of each color segment in the boxes on the next page. There are no wrong answers.

Number of red segments: [ ]     Number of green segments: [ ]

How did you do? The number of colored boxes will give you
an idea of your mental health right now. Read on to find out...

### More red segments

Are you struggling with your mental health at the moment, and
feeling worried or stressed? What is it about those things you
did today that made you feel like that? Take things one step at a
time and look at one red segment to start with. Try writing down
everything about it that bothered you. Can you change anything
to make things better? It also may help to talk to an adult and
ask for their help and advice.

### More green segments

Your mental health is in a good place, and you have a positive
outlook on life. Keep doing what you are doing. If you had some
red segments, ask yourself if there's anything you could change
to make those activities more enjoyable. Think of a happy person
close to you and imagine how they would deal with it.

### Equal red and green segments

Your mental health is fine with some things, but you struggle
with others. Think about how you can work on the red segments
to turn them green. Can you look at things in the red segments
in a different way? Make a list of any positive things, and things
that you can be grateful for with them. It may help to talk to an
adult and ask for their help or advice.

# WORRY MONSTER

This Monster has a strange appetite, as she loves to eat worries!

*Let go of your worries by drawing anything that is bothering you on the plate. Watch how fast the worry monster gobbles them up!*

BURRRP!

# MENTAL HEALTH TOOL KIT

Cheering yourself up can help to turn those worries into no worries.

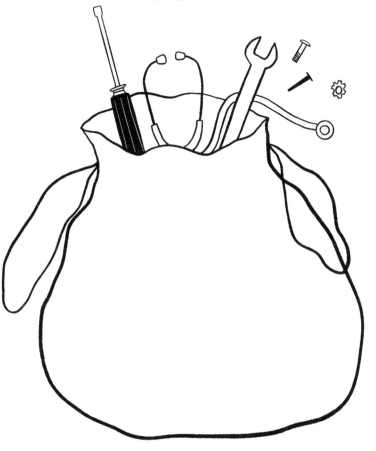

*What things can you do to cheer up and improve your mental health? Think of things that make you feel happy and calm. Write them in this tool kit.*

# ALL ABOUT ME

You are unique and special as there is no one else like you on the planet.

*Draw or write your favorite things that are special to you.*

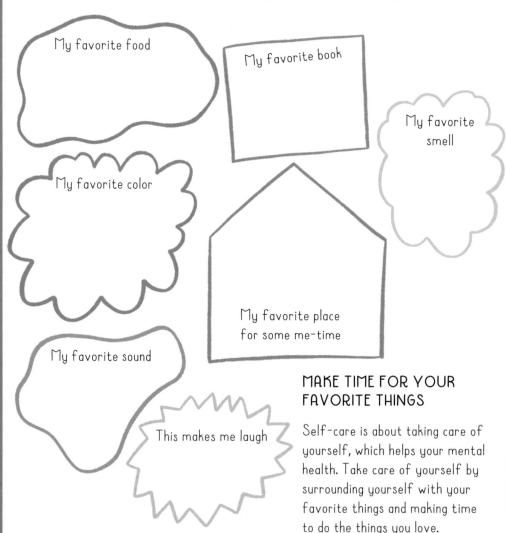

My favorite food

My favorite book

My favorite smell

My favorite color

My favorite place for some me-time

My favorite sound

This makes me laugh

## MAKE TIME FOR YOUR FAVORITE THINGS

Self-care is about taking care of yourself, which helps your mental health. Take care of yourself by surrounding yourself with your favorite things and making time to do the things you love.

# FEELING GOOD

Give a shout-out to all the good things
that have happened in your week.

*Write one good thing in each space.
Include anything that has made you smile.*

# TALKING HELPS

It helps our mental health to talk about our feelings.

It is also a good idea to talk to a parent, caregiver, teacher, or friend if you are worried about anything. Trying to ignore feelings or dealing with problems on your own is not the answer. Taking a step toward talking to someone will release some of the stress and you will feel better in the end.

## A STEP IN THE RIGHT DIRECTION

Color in the steps to show you are ready to talk to someone right now.

## WHAT MAKES A GOOD LISTENER?

☆ Listens to what I have to say
☆ Doesn't judge me
☆ Is calm
☆ Supports me
☆ I can trust them

*Can you be a good listener for a friend or someone in your family?*

## PEOPLE I CAN TALK TO

*Draw or write down six people you could talk to about your feelings and worries. If you can't think of that many, don't worry, one is all you need.*

# REWIRING THE BRAIN WITH POSITIVITY

Being positive will help you to lead a happy, healthy life.

Your brain changes all the time—scientists call this "plastic" because you can make plastic into all sorts of shapes. Because it is plastic, you can train your brain to be more positive! Your brain is continually checking over your thoughts. If you have more negative thoughts, then your brain creates stress and sadness in your body. But if you have more positive thoughts, your brain creates relaxation and happiness. So, the trick is to replace negative thoughts with positive thoughts to rewire your brain. The more you practice this, the easier being positive will become.

Treat yourself to something you love doing.

## WAYS TO REWIRE YOUR BRAIN WITH POSITIVE POWER

Follow every negative thought with a positive thought.

Look for the positive in situations and people.

Change the way you look at things: see something difficult as a challenge.

Find a less stressful, more positive, way to do things that cause you stress.

Plan a few positive things to fill your day.

Make some happy habits to fill your day.

Think of three things you are grateful for at the start or end of a day.

## BE TRUE TO YOURSELF

It's okay if you don't feel in a positive mood all the time, as it's normal to feel down in the dumps at times. Take care to focus on positive things you really believe in, rather than trying to convince yourself to feel positive about something that has really upset you, as this can leave you feeling more stressed.

# POSITIVE TWIST

We all have a critical, negative voice inside
our heads from time to time.

Look at how these negative thoughts have been turned into positive thoughts.
Then write down some of your own negative thoughts as you have them, and
think of how you can reframe them in a positive way.

I can't do this.

I'm never going to get all this done.

No one likes me.

I give up!

- - - - - - - - - - - - - - - - -

- - - - - - - - - - - - - - - - -

- - - - - - - - - - - - - - - - -

- - - - - - - - - - - - - - - - -

I'm learning and mistakes are part of learning.

I can take it one step at a time.

Think of three people who do like me.

Can I try it another way?

- - - - - - - - - - - - - - - - -

- - - - - - - - - - - - - - - - -

- - - - - - - - - - - - - - - - -

- - - - - - - - - - - - - - - - -

## WHY DON'T YOU...

...make this Jar of Positivity to put in your positive thoughts?
Any time you are feeling negative, pull out a positive thought
from the jar and see if it helps to lift your mood.

JAR OF
POSITIVITY

# POSITIVITY POSTER

I am
STRONG
I am
Loved

Make a positive poster full of positive
words and sayings.

*Write the words in different colors, sizes, and styles. You
could also add some doodles. Hang it up where you can see
it every day, and read it out often to remind yourself how
great you are.*

*Here are some suggestions
for things you may include.*

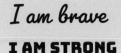

I am brave

I AM STRONG

I am Loved

I AM UNIQUE

POSITIVE

Grateful

STRONG

BRILLIANT

# LOVE TREE

Love is an emotion that fills us with joy.

Both giving and receiving love is essential to our happiness. Fill these hearts with pictures of people and things you love. Don't forget to include yourself, as you are special and loved, too.

# MINDFULNESS

You may have heard of mindfulness, but what does it mean and how does it make us happy?

Mindfulness means that the mind is fully attending to what is happening both inside and outside our bodies in the moment. When we are mindful, we are aware of our thoughts, feelings, body, and surroundings in the present.

Accept

BE AWARE

Let go

Focus

Be present

JUST BE

Relax

It is normal for our minds to wander, as we go over things that have happened in the past and think about things coming up in the future. But all of these thoughts can overload our minds and make us feel restless and anxious. Focusing on the moment calms the mind and stops it from drifting off. A calm mind is a happy mind.

## WAYS TO BE MINDFUL

Meditation is one way to calm the mind. In meditation, a person stops what they are doing, sits quietly, and focuses their mind on the present moment. Check out some meditation exercises on later pages.

Being grateful for things helps us to appreciate things as they happen, at that moment. Little things such as a smile, seeing friends, the sun shining through a window after days of rain, ice cream, visiting grandparents. Noticing and delighting in things we see, feel, hear, taste, and smell as they happen is part of being grateful.

These are some of the ways mindfulness makes our lives better:

GET MORE DONE

BETTER CONCENTRATION

FEEL CALMER

SLEEP BETTER

MORE POSITIVE

HAPPIER

### Practice, Practice, Practice

It's normal for our minds to race ahead, thinking of other things, but the more you practice mindfulness, the better you will become, and the calmer and happier you will feel. Practice being mindful throughout your day and set aside a quiet time to practice some mindfulness.

# BEING MINDFUL

Give these simple, mindful activities a go. Make sure you are not distracted by anything when you do them. Turn off any phones, televisions, and computers, and find a quiet place.

## MINDFUL SEEING

*Sketch an everyday object with a pencil. Find something small with interesting detail such as a leaf, stone, or shell.*

Things to notice:
- ☆ Are there any dark shadows or highlights?
- ☆ Do you notice any patterns, such as swirls, curls, or zigzags?
- ☆ What shape is it?
- ☆ Is it smooth or rough?

## MINDFUL LISTENING

*Close your eyes and ask someone to make a noise with something. For example, banging a spoon inside a pan, crinkling a wrapper, or running their fingers over a comb.*

Things to notice:
- ☆ How does it sound?
- ☆ Does it clank, crinkle, bang, rattle, or make some other sound?
- ☆ Can you guess what it is?
- ☆ Does it make you think of anything else?

## MINDFUL EATING

*Put a mouthful of food that you like in your mouth. Close your eyes and chew the food slowly, paying attention to every bite and savoring the taste.*

Things to notice:
- ☆ How does it taste? Is it bitter, sweet, salty, meaty, or some other taste?
- ☆ What does it feel like in your mouth?
- ☆ Does your mouth water?
- ☆ How does the rest of your body feel?

## MINDFUL SMELLING

*Close your eyes and ask someone to put something with a strong smell in front of you. It may be an orange, cheese, or something safe from outside, such as a flower or blade of grass.*

**Things to notice:**

☆ How does it smell? Is it sweet, minty, fruity, woody, or some other smell?

☆ Can you guess what it is?

☆ Does it make you think of anything else?

☆ How does the rest of your body feel?

## MINDFUL FEELING (MOVING)

*Get up for this and pretend you are walking in rainboots along a slippery, muddy, sloping path. Pay attention to your movement, noticing how you lift up your feet and how you hold your body.*

**Things to notice:**

☆ Can you pick up each foot easily? Do you put each foot down slowly?

☆ Do you use your arms to help you balance?

☆ Are you standing up straight, or leaning forward?

☆ Is there a difference between walking mindfully and normal walking?

*Did you notice while you were being mindful that you forgot about other things that had been on your mind?*

*Was it easier to listen, taste and smell with your eyes closed? If yes or no, why do you think that is?*

"*Be happy in the moment, that's enough. Each moment is all we need, not more.*"

Mother Teresa

Let your mind wander and fill this space with happy things.

# MINDFUL MAZE

Trace with a pencil round this mindful maze, being careful not to touch the line edges. If you touch an edge stop for a few seconds, close your eyes, focus on your breathing, and have a mindful moment.
Then continue.

This is not a race, so do it mindfully. Take your time and enjoy the activity.

# A MOMENT OF CALM

Breathing gets more oxygen into your blood, which opens up your blood vessels and calms you down. Try this breathing meditation exercise the next time you feel stressed. A friend can read out the instructions for you, then swap.

**1.** Sit in a comfortable position. Many people sit cross-legged on the floor, while others sit on a chair. You need to be able to relax, but also to stay awake. Gently rest your hands on your knees. Sit up straight and hold your head up, but stay relaxed.

**2.** Close your eyes and relax. Slowly breathe in and out. Let go of any tension in your face, your shoulders or anywhere you feel it. Pay attention to your breathing... in and out, in and out.

**3.** Don't worry if your mind wanders. Each time you have a thought, just imagine it floating away, and bring yourself back to focus on your breathing.

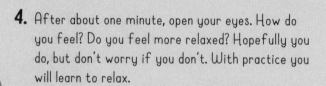

**4.** After about one minute, open your eyes. How do you feel? Do you feel more relaxed? Hopefully you do, but don't worry if you don't. With practice you will learn to relax.

# SAY THANKS

Write a letter to the Universe thanking it for all the things you are grateful for in your life.

You may choose some of these, or have some different ones of your own:
friends • family
pets • home
school • health

Dear Universe, I am grateful for

From

How do you feel after writing your letter? Do you feel in a good place? Being grateful helps us to focus on happy things.

# CHILL OUT

We pack a lot into our lives and our days can get busy with school work, chores, homework, seeing friends and family. If we are not careful, we may feel stressed-out from doing too much. Every now and then it's good to stop and give yourself some "me time," so you can chill out and recharge your batteries.

Draw how you like to chill out here.

# HAVE A HUG

Draw your face in the frame and give yourself a big, cuddly bear hug—you deserve it!

# WHAT IS RESILIENCE?

"I'll never learn all these notes!"

"I will learn one note at a time."

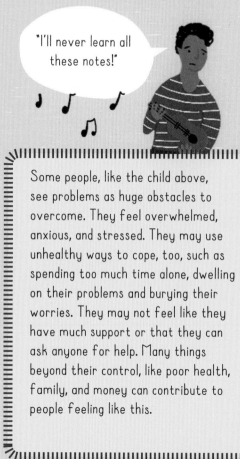

Some people, like the child above, see problems as huge obstacles to overcome. They feel overwhelmed, anxious, and stressed. They may use unhealthy ways to cope, too, such as spending too much time alone, dwelling on their problems and burying their worries. They may not feel like they have much support or that they can ask anyone for help. Many things beyond their control, like poor health, family, and money can contribute to people feeling like this.

Other people, like the child here, have a more positive reaction, dealing with problems face-on. They may still feel stressed and anxious, but they have the mental tools to cope with their problems and get over them, without falling apart. Importantly, these people are likely have a strong support network of family and friends who they can turn to, and know that they can ask for help.

## BOUNCING BACK

Resilient people bounce back and recover more quickly from setbacks. They don't expect everything to be perfect and can accept that it's okay to not feel okay at times, and can work through uncomfortable feelings. They also don't put themselves down every time they make a mistake, as they realise that mistakes are part of learning.

# BUILD YOUR RESILIENCE

Don't worry if you struggle with your mental tools.
The good news is you can work on your resilience.

## CHANGE YOUR THINKING

It's no use worrying about things you can't change, such as something that's already happened. But you **can** change how you react to it. Take a step back from the problem—if you can, walk away for a few minutes and take some deep breaths to calm down. Then, instead of reacting emotionally to the problem with phrases such as "I can't cope with this," or "It's not fair," look at the problem through someone else's eyes. For example, imagine you are an alien who has just landed on Earth and are faced with this problem. What would the alien say? How would the alien react?

## FOCUS ON THE POSITIVE THINGS

Can you try and reframe a problem as a challenge? Can you find any positive things about it? This may help you to feel better, or even find a solution. Try to see it as an opportunity to challenge yourself and develop new skills.

## BE REALISTIC

Try not to put pressure on yourself to do everything perfectly. If you make a mistake, don't let it knock you down, but learn and grow from it. Some of the most amazing discoveries in science have come from mistakes!

## SMALL STEPS

Rather than looking at the whole problem and feeling overwhelmed, start by tackling a small part of it. When that's done, tackle the next small part. Before long, you'll find that you've conquered it!

## ASK FOR HELP

We all need help from time to time. It's courageous to admit that you are struggling and to ask for help. Talking about our problems can also help us to look at things in other ways and see ways around them.

# BE CURIOUS

It helps to talk to others to find out how they overcome challenges and their ways of coping. Pretend you are a reporter and interview your family and friends. Ask them to tell you about a challenge they have faced and the steps they took to overcome it.

*Draw the person you are interviewing.*

Name: _____
Challenge: _____
_____
_____
Steps: _____
_____
_____

Name: _____
Challenge: _____
_____
_____
Steps: _____
_____
_____

Name: _____
Challenge: _____
_____
_____
Steps: _____
_____
_____

**STEP ONE**

**STEP TWO**

**STEP THREE**

**STEP FOUR**

**STEP FIVE**

MY CHALLENGE IS . . .

# SMALL STEPS

Are you ready for a challenge? Learning a new skill is not easy and can be challenging. Think of something new you would love to learn and the small steps you can take to learn it. Maybe you want to learn an instrument or a craft, or something simpler such as how to wiggle your ears, or do a magic trick?

"I'm mighty!"

Write down your challenge and five small steps that you can take to learn it.

Ask yourself: "What is one little thing I can do to start?" Then when you've done that and are ready, plan your next step. You can take as many steps as you want —use a blank sheet of paper and draw some more footprints if you need to.

# HELPFUL HATS

The next time you face a challenge try this Helpful Hats technique to tackle it. You will need four different colored hats, or make some colored paper hats.

### MAKE A PAPER HAT

To make four paper hats you will need four different colored sheets of rectangular paper: one sheet for each hat. Or you can use newspaper that you've painted.

**1.** Fold the paper in half lengthways, then unfold it.

**2.** Fold the top of the paper down in half towards you.

**3.** Fold each corner over as in the picture.

**4.** Fold up a flap on each side to make the rim of the hat.

Now you are ready to turn your hats into Helpful Hats . . .

### STEPS

1. Assign a question to each hat. Always keep the same color hat with the same question, so that hat is always linked to that question. Color the small hats to show which question each hat stands for.

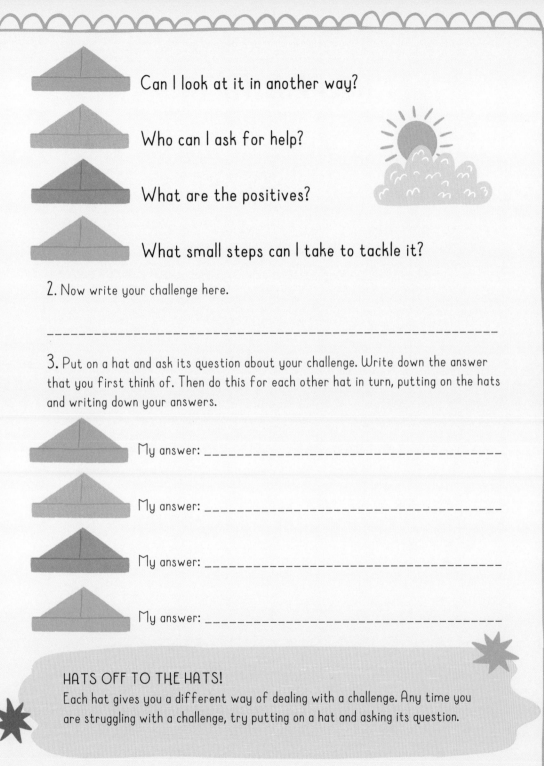

Can I look at it in another way?

Who can I ask for help?

What are the positives?

What small steps can I take to tackle it?

2. Now write your challenge here.

_____

3. Put on a hat and ask its question about your challenge. Write down the answer that you first think of. Then do this for each other hat in turn, putting on the hats and writing down your answers.

My answer: _____

My answer: _____

My answer: _____

My answer: _____

HATS OFF TO THE HATS!
Each hat gives you a different way of dealing with a challenge. Any time you are struggling with a challenge, try putting on a hat and asking its question.

# FAILING

We all experience failure and make mistakes. Maybe you have lost a game, done badly in a test, not been picked for a team, struggled to work something out, or answered a question incorrectly. How did it make you feel?

## HEALTHY WAYS TO COPE WITH FAILURE

Failure is not a nice feeling as it creates painful emotions, which is why we don't like to fail. But did you know that failure helps our brains to grow? Through failing we learn new things, which is why it's good to step out of our comfort zones. The key to keeping our good mental health, is learning to cope with failure in a healthy way. Here are some healthy ways to deal with failure:

## ACCEPT YOUR EMOTIONS

Accept how a failure makes you feel, instead of trying to cover up or ignore any feelings. It may be one of the feelings above or another one. Know that it's okay to feel that way.

## GIVE YOURSELF SOME SELF-CARE

Now that you have accepted how you feel, treat yourself to something special that helps when you feel down. It may be curling up in a quiet place with your favorite magazine, cuddling a pet, watching a funny movie with your family, or chatting to a friend. Resist comforting yourself with unhealthy things such as eating sweet things, as these will not help your body.

## CHANGE NEGATIVE THOUGHTS INTO POSITIVE THOUGHTS

It's easy to think you failed because you were no good, and to doubt if you will ever succeed. But these negative thoughts don't make any sense. Think of the positive things, such as how you tried your best (which is all you can do). Try not to let one failure sum up what you think of yourself.

## WHAT CAN YOU LEARN FROM YOUR FAILURE?

Ask yourself what things you have learned from your failure. Can you make a plan for next time, rather than dwelling on your mistakes? Are there any things you could do differently to change the result?

### GREAT INVENTIONS FROM MISTAKES

☆ Fireworks

☆ Microwave oven

☆ X-rays

☆ Penicillin

☆ Post-it notes

☆ Chewing gum

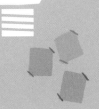

Richard James invented the Slinky toy by accident. He was an engineer working with springs, when he accidentally knocked some springs off a shelf. He was amazed at how they gracefully "walked" instead of falling flat on the floor.

"The most certain way to succeed is always to try just one more time."

Thomas Edison

Let your mind wander and fill this space with happy things.

# OUR PLANET EARTH

**We all live on and share
one planet - Earth.**

Anywhere you are in the world, you
feel the same warm sun, chilly rain
and gentle breezes, and look up
at the same marvelous moon and
twinkling stars. All over the world
amazing plants push their way up
through soil and unfold their leaves
to grow shiny berries, plump fruit,
and bright flowers. There are wild
animals with sharp claws, fabulous fur,
twitching noses, tusks, and tails. And
there are so many of us ... all shapes
and sizes, young and old, with smiles and
laughs, troubles and worries.

Taking time to be grateful for our planet and
every living thing on it is good for our mental
health. It grounds us by reminding us that we are a tiny
part of something much bigger than ourselves. Spiritual
people believe that we are part of something divine, meaning
connected to a god. What do you believe?

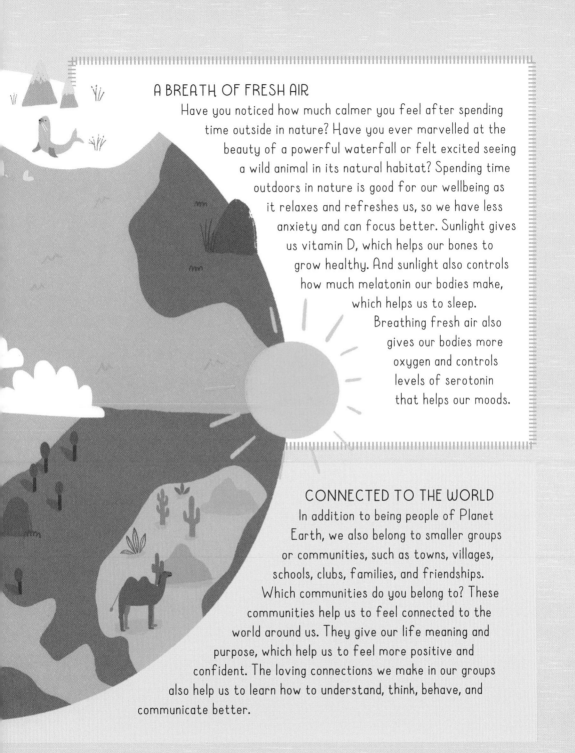

## A BREATH OF FRESH AIR

Have you noticed how much calmer you feel after spending time outside in nature? Have you ever marvelled at the beauty of a powerful waterfall or felt excited seeing a wild animal in its natural habitat? Spending time outdoors in nature is good for our wellbeing as it relaxes and refreshes us, so we have less anxiety and can focus better. Sunlight gives us vitamin D, which helps our bones to grow healthy. And sunlight also controls how much melatonin our bodies make, which helps us to sleep.

Breathing fresh air also gives our bodies more oxygen and controls levels of serotonin that helps our moods.

## CONNECTED TO THE WORLD

In addition to being people of Planet Earth, we also belong to smaller groups or communities, such as towns, villages, schools, clubs, families, and friendships. Which communities do you belong to? These communities help us to feel connected to the world around us. They give our life meaning and purpose, which help us to feel more positive and confident. The loving connections we make in our groups also help us to learn how to understand, think, behave, and communicate better.

# IN A WONDERFUL SPIN

Planet Earth is very special. Follow the clues and find fourteen wonderful things in the word spiral that can be found on our planet. The last letter of each word is the first letter of the next word.

Here's an example
Word spiral: thunderiver
Clues: weather, water.
The words are thunder and river.

Add some more words to complete the spiral. Remember the rule that the last letter of a word is the first letter of the next.

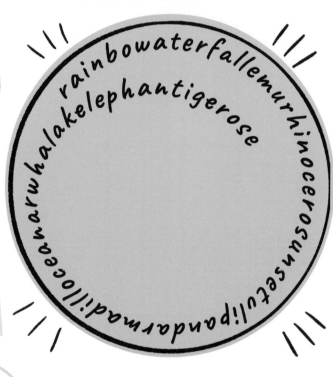

rainbowaterfallemurhinocerosunsetulipandarwadilloceanarwhalakelephantigerose

Clues to the words in order: weather, water, animal, animal, weather, flower, animal, animal, water, animal, water, animal, animal, flower.

# READ ALL ABOUT IT!

Write a story for a newspaper about how wonderful the village, town, or city you live in is. Write about the plants, animals, and people that you see there. Describe the buildings and any interesting places, and what you like about them.
You want your readers to love the place as much as you do, so use lots of positive and happy words.

You may choose to use some of these words: AMAZING, ASTONISHING, FABULOUS, FANTASTIC, HAPPY, MAGNIFICENT, MARVELOUS, SENSATIONAL, TERRIFIC, WONDERFUL.

*THE*

## WEEKLY

Add the name of where you live here.

Draw a picture of where you live.

Write your name here.

# NATURE BINGO

Go on a mindful walk and see if you can spot these things—check the box in each square as you spot it. Make it into a game and do it with a friend and see who is the first to spot them.

SMALL BIRD

RED FLOWER

BLOSSOM

SPIDER

EARTHWORM

LOG

RAINBOW

WATER BIRD

SQUIRREL

# NATURE POEM

Go outside and try writing a short mindful poem like the one here about things you see, hear, smell, or feel in nature.

High up in the oak
The animals are busy
Scritch, scratch, tap, tap, tap.

This three-lined poem is called a haiku, which is a type of poem that originates from Japan. Read it out loud and tap out the syllables. It has five syllables in the first and third lines, and seven syllables in the middle line.

# TERRIFIC TREES

Trees are good for our planet and us. Take a moment to stop by a tree: what do you see, feel, smell, and hear? Do you feel calmer? Trees shelter us from the rain and shade us from the hot sun. They also provide food, wood for building, oxygen to breathe, and they clean carbon dioxide from the air. You can identify different types of trees just by looking at their leaves.

*See if you can spot these trees on a walk. Check the boxes when you find them.*

☐ oak    ☐ horse chestnut    ☐ beech    ☐ black poplar

☐ sycamore    ☐ birch

☐ wild cherry    ☐ hawthorn    ☐ hazel    ☐ ash

## WHY DON'T YOU...

... Sadly, so many trees are being chopped down in the world. But you can make a difference by asking an adult to help you plant a tree. Perhaps you could speak to your school about doing a tree planting project. The best time to plant one is between October and April. Make sure you do your research first by checking out things such as how big the tree will grow and what soil it likes.

Use this space
to color in all the
different types of
leaves you see.

# RECYCLE IT!

Recycling things, instead of throwing them away, is one way of being kind to our planet. Here's an idea for recycling an old juice or milk carton by turning it into a bird feeder. It helps the birds as well as the planet!

**1.** Wash the carton when it's empty. Draw a door on the front and back of the carton. Then use scissors to cut out the doors .

**2.** Next draw a wing on each side. You can ask an adult to help you cut the wings —don't cut the top edge of the wing as it needs to stay attached.

**3.** Paint your feeder (child-friendly PVA paints work well). When it's dry, paint on a face.

**4.** Ask an adult to help you punch a hole in the top edge of the carton with a hole punch. Thread some string through the hole.

**5.** Fill your feeder with bird seed.

**6.** Ask an adult to help you hang it up. Sit back and watch who comes to visit.

# CARING FOR MY PLANET

Our planet is very special as it
is our home. It is important to look
after it for ourselves and the people
who will live after us.

## WALK MORE

Draw one thing you can
do to help care for our
planet. Look at past
pages, and the words and
pictures here for ideas.

*Recycle*

## RE-USE

# GETTING TO KNOW YOU

Our community of family and friends help us to feel loved and supported, by listening to us and being interested in our lives.

*Do this quiz with a friend or someone in your family to find out how well you know each other by answering each question for both of you. Then check your answers with each other at the end and count up how many you scored.*

| QUESTION | ME | FRIEND / FAMILY |
|---|---|---|
| 1. What is their favorite color? | | |
| 2. How do they relax? | | |
| 3. What is their favorite food? | | |
| 4. Name something they are good at. | | |
| 5. Describe what they were wearing yesterday (or when you last saw them). | | |
| 6. If they're a kid, what do they want to be when they grow up, if an adult, what do they do now? | | |

**If you scored 1 to 3:**
Err, is this really your friend/family member or a chimp you once met in a zoo?! It's time to spend more quality time with this person. Preferably with a pen and paper to hand.

**If you scored 4 to 6:**
You know your friend or family member very well. Keep up with the listening and paying attention.

*Relationships are give and take: it is important for us to support our family and friends, too.*

# FRIENDSHIP PAPER CHAIN

Let your friends know how much you appreciate them
by making them a friendship paper chain.

To make a chain of four friends you will need:
- A strip of paper, at least 12 in. long
  and 4 in. wide • Pencil
- Colored pencils/pens • Scissors

1. Place your strip of paper so the two
   long sides are on the top and bottom.
   Fold the paper in half as shown.
   Then fold the paper in half again.

2. Draw a friend on the top of the
   folded paper. Make sure the ends
   of the hands go off each side.
   Use the template if you need to.

3. Cut through all the layers of paper
   to cut out your friend shape.

4. Unfold your chain of friends. Color
   each friend, adding a face and clothes
   on the front. Write a name and one
   happy word that describes them on
   the back of each friend.

   *To make more than four friends,*
   *use a longer strip of paper and*
   *fold it over more times.*

USE AS A GUIDE
TO FILL PAPER

KIND    FUNNY    FRIENDLY    THOUGHTFUL

# SPREADING KINDNESS

When people are kind to us it makes us feel happy.
When we are kind to others, this also makes us feel happy.
We can all make time in our busy lives to show kindness to
each other and spread some happiness. Here are some
ways you can make a difference in people's lives.

## KINDNESS STONES
Paint messages and symbols of kindness on stones,
and leave them outside for people to find.

## SAVE THE PENNIES
Save some of your pocket money
in a special jar to donate to a charity.

My pocket money for others

## TWO KIND WORDS
Say thank you to someone you don't usually thank,
but who helps you. Such as your teacher, a parent,
or a brother or sister.

## CLEAR-OUT
Have a clear-out of some good toys and clothes that
you can give to someone who might need them more.

TOYS

## VOLUNTEERING
Find out if there are events where you live that
you can volunteer to take part in. For example,
picking litter or planting trees.

## SPONSORED EVENT

Can you do a sponsored event and give the money you raise to a charity? What would you do ... swimming, walking, running?

*Plan a week of kindness and write one kind thing you can do for someone else each day.*

*Check the heart when you have done it.*

## MY KIND WEEK

MONDAY --------------------------------------- ♥

TUESDAY -------------------------------------- ♥

WEDNESDAY ------------------------------------ ♥

THURSDAY ------------------------------------- ♥

FRIDAY --------------------------------------- ♥

SATURDAY ------------------------------------- ♥

SUNDAY --------------------------------------- ♥

"There are only two ways to live your life. One is as though nothing is a miracle. The other is as though everything is a miracle."

Albert Einstein

Let your mind wander and fill this space with happy things.

# BEING CREATIVE

Doing something creative makes you feel good
as you can put your heart into your creations.
It is a wonderful, safe way to express yourself
and have a voice.

## CREATIVE ACTIVITIES
*Can you add a few more creative
activities that you enjoy?*

PAINTING

WRITING

DANCING

ACTING

## SHOW YOUR EMOTIONS
Being creative is a good way of expressing your emotions
and coping with your feelings. For example, the next time
you feel upset, try dipping a paintbrush into a rich, dark
blue paint and swishing it across the paper in big, wavy
strokes to paint a stormy sea. Does that help you to feel
better? With art you can show how you feel on the inside.
Expressing things you are not comfortable with sharing is
often easier to show through a painting.

## CREATIVE THINKING

Did you know that creative thinking is good for our brains as it helps them to grow? For example, all that mind mapping of ideas and solving problems as we create things, makes new pathways in our brains. Trying new things and taking risks also helps to build resilience, as it pushes you out of your comfort zone. Find something new to create every day!

*Flex your creative thinking muscles and think of eight more things a simple comb could be turned into. Free your imagination and think wild!*

1. Spikes on a dinosaur's back

2. An alien's feeler

3. _____

4. _____

5. _____

6. _____

7. _____

8. _____

9. _____

10. _____

## LIFE SKILLS

Being creative and letting your imagination run free, for example, through storytelling, games, and music, gives you many life skills, including expressing yourself, solving problems, and confidence. It also helps you to see the world in new ways and appreciate different ideas and cultures. It helps you to feel fulfilled and happy.

# WILDEST DREAMS

What things do you really love doing? What places make your heart sing? The park, the seaside, the movies, or a bowling alley? What things inspire you? Music, colors, sparkly things, or animals? There are no wrong answers. These are things that are special to YOU. They are YOUR passions.

It's good to have passions as they make us happy and give our lives a purpose and a focus. Some passions are small, such as one thing you are burning to do that day. Other passions are big, such as dreams of playing the piano in front of a big crowd to huge applause.

*Draw one of your wildest dreams in the mist from the genie's lamp. See the next page for tips on how to make your dream come true.*

# MAKE IT HAPPEN

It's great to have dreams, but as a seed needs soil and water to grow, your passions need your care and attention to blossom. Even things that we love doing, or want in our lives, need working at. It helps to set goals and deadlines to break up the things we want into small, realistic parts that we can achieve.

*Write one of your dreams in the plant (it may be the dream you drew opposite), and three small goals and deadlines that you can take to make it happen, underneath.*

My dream is

Ideas for goals:
☆ Practice 20 minutes every day.
☆ Talk to friends with the same passion.
☆ Find a club I can join.
☆ Finish part of it by next week.

GOAL: ........................................................................

.......................................... Deadline : ..................
(daily, by next week, by next month)

**Why don't you**
*Make a Life Board to show things you want to have and achieve in your life? Cut out pictures from magazines, stick on photos, draw, and write anything that inspires you and fills you with joy. Put it somewhere where you can see it to remind you of your goals.*

MY LIFE BOARD

FRIENDS

FAMILY

# WHAT DREAMS ARE MADE OF

Be creative with your colors and enjoy the moment
as you draw what you think dreams are made of.

# COMEDY SCHOOL

Have you noticed how good you feel after a fit of the giggles? Laughing is good for us as it increases the endorphins in our bodies, which as we have seen earlier, make us feel happy. Scientists have also shown that laughter can help ease pain and even increase our immunity. And there's nothing like a big belly laugh to give our tummy muscles and hearts a good workout!

## WHAT MAKES YOU LAUGH?
Write down five things that make you laugh.

☆ ......................................................................
☆ ......................................................................
☆ ......................................................................
☆ ......................................................................
☆ ......................................................................

## SEE THE FUNNY SIDE
Some things are serious and are not to be made fun of, but being able to see the funny side of things can help us to deal with them. For example, it's embarrassing to stumble on the stage in a school play, but if you can laugh at yourself later, that can help to take away any negative emotions such as anger that you may be feeling. And even when you are in an awkward situation, such as showing up to a party as the only one who dressed up, if you can laugh at it, it will be much less stressful.

## JOIN IN THE FUN
Have you found that when one friend gets the giggles, it can set you off laughing? And if you're not careful, it can spread to the whole group, and soon you're all clutching your sides laughing. Laughing is infectious and helps us to connect with others. The more laughter you bring into your life, the more you will help to raise the mood of those around you and the happier you will all feel.

# TONGUE TWISTERS

Tongue twisters do what they say—they get your tongue in a twist, especially when you try to say them quickly!

*Read the tongue twisters below out loud as fast as you can a few times. Color in a tongue to show if you have a super twisty tongue or your tongue is tied in knots.*

Tongue-tied     Talented twister

Red lorry, yellow lorry. ...........................................

A proper copper, coffee pot. ...............................

The slippery seal slowly slid sideways. .....................

The cheeky chimp chewed on chips. ...........................

The plucky duck drove a mucky truck. .....................

## WRITE YOUR OWN TONGUE TWISTERS
The trick with writing a tongue twister is to use words with the same first letter and sounds. Look at the pictures and try writing your own tongue twisters to describe them. Challenge your friends to say your tongue twisters out loud, as fast as they can.

----------------------------------------

----------------------------------------

A llama!

----------------------------------------

----------------------------------------

# GIGGLETIME

We all love watching funny characters, for example in cartoons, and reading about them in books. But what makes them funny?

Some may have exaggerated features such as an over-sized nose, huge feet, or an extra-long, curly moustache. Others may have strange things about them such as wearing odd socks, a tiny hat too small for their head, or trousers so baggy that a bird has built its nest in them!

*Be as silly as you dare and draw a funny character here. Make sure to give your character a name once you've finished.*

# FUNNY FORFEITS

Let your hair down and play this game of funny forfeits with friends or family.

## HOW TO PLAY

You will need two dice and at least two players, but more can play.

1. Agree how long you will play the game for, so the game ends when the time is up.
2. Take it in turns to roll the two dice and add up the total.
3. Do the forfeit with the matching total.
4. If you throw a double number, lucky you! Choose a forfeit for a friend to do, instead of you. Continue the game as if you have had a turn.

## POSSIBLE FORFEITS:

| 2 | 3 | 4 |
|---|---|---|
| DO A FUNNY WALK. | DO YOUR BEST IMPRESSION OF SOMEONE. | SING THE LYRICS OF ONE SONG TO THE TUNE OF ANOTHER. |
| **5** | **6** | **7** |
| TELL A JOKE. | ACT OUT A SCENE FROM A FILM, PLAYING ALL THE PARTS. | TELL A FUNNY STORY ABOUT A SAUSAGE DOG. |
| **8** | **9** | **10** |
| PUT ON AS MANY CLOTHES AS YOU CAN IN A MINUTE. | SHOW OFF YOUR BEST DANCE MOVES. | LAUGH FOR 30 SECONDS. |

| 11 | 12 |
|---|---|
| DRAW A PICTURE USING YOUR TOES. | DOUBLE NUMBER: PASS A FORFEIT ON. |

# DOODLE DANCE

The animals love dressing up and throwing shapes on the dance floor to the Dizzy Doodles' music. Draw some crazy animals having fun at the Doodle Dance.

"No one is you and that is your biggest power."

Dave Grohl

Let your mind wander and fill this space with happy things.

# YOU CAN'T BE HAPPY ALL THE TIME

We have seen how a positive attitude and leading a healthy life with good food, sleep, exercise, self-care, and goals helps us to be happy. But no one is happy all the time. Happiness is something we have to work at throughout our lives, to create a way of life that brings us happiness and fulfilment. If you struggle with happiness, the good news is that by taking small steps you can start changing things right now.

## WHAT IF YOU FEEL BAD?

If you are feeling bad, the first step is to accept what you are feeling rather than trying to bury any uncomfortable feelings. For example, say "I am feeling sad" or "I am angry about that" or "My feelings are hurt." When we admit how we are feeling, we can then try the next step, which is to find ways of coping with those feelings by managing them.

Sometimes our feelings can feel big, uncontrollable and confusing, and we don't know what to do with them. In these moments you might make some bad choices before you learn to make some better ones. That's okay. It takes time to understand your feelings and find healthy ways of managing them.

## TRY NOT TO LET YOUR FEELINGS HOLD YOU BACK

Just because you feel uncomfortable about something, so long as it's safe, it doesn't always mean it's bad for you. For example, if you feel nervous about going to a school dance, try not to let those feelings stop you from going. Tell your friends or parents how you feel, and with their support find some courage to go. Stepping out of your comfort zone will help you to feel more confident and proud of yourself.

## FIND YOUR SUPERHERO

If you are feeling really bad talk to a parent, caregiver, or teacher and ask for their help. We all need to find our inner brave superhero and ask for help at times.

# FURTHER RESOURCES

Check out these links to find out even more information about emotions and mental health.

www.actionforhappiness.org
www.seizetheawkward.org
www.youngminds.org.uk
www.childmind.org
www.thetrevorproject.org
www.atlasofemotions.org
www.kooth.com
www.headspace.com

You can also contact a free and confidential helpline that is available online or by phone, such as:

Childhelp
(1-800) 422-4453
www.childhelp.org

Crisis text line
Text 741741
www.crisistextline.org

Stomp out bullying
www.stompoutbullying.org